Tuning
Yachts & Small Keelboats

Fernhurst Books

Tuning
Yachts & Small Keelboats

Lawrie Smith

First published in 1988 by
Fernhurst Books, Dukes Path, High Street, Arundel,
West Sussex, BN18 9AJ, England

ISBN 0 906754 35 6

Acknowledgements

The publishers would like to thank Warwick
Collins for the loan of *Fighter*, John Warren for
the loan of his J24 *Endeavour*, and Lawrie Smith,
Rodney Pattisson, Ross Francis, Bob Wylie and
Christine Graves for crewing the boats in the
photo sessions. Peter Newbury kindly loaned his
Sigma 33 *Joker* from which the pictures were
taken.

Photographs

The photographs are by Tim Hore, with the
exception of the following:
Hamo Thorneycroft Marine Photography: page 65.
Yachting Photographics: pages 2-3, 11, 14, 21,
28-29, 32, 39, 40, 42, 45, 46, 58, 66, 69, 70, 75, 82,
85, 86, 91, 93, 95.

Design by John Woodward.
Composition by A&G Phototypesetters, Knaphill.
Artwork by PanTek, Maidstone.

Printed in Hong Kong through World Print Limited

Contents

Introduction   6

Assembling the gear   8

Tuning the rig   16

Tuning the genoa   28

Tuning the mainsail   49

Upwind faultfinder   61

Fractional rig problems   74

Reaching   70

Running   88

Major surgery   92

Introduction

For centuries sailors have been trying to make their boats go faster. Nothing is more annoying than watching a similar boat pull ahead, and many people despair of making their own boats match the speed of the champion's. Yet there are always good reasons why one boat is slower than another. Finding those reasons and doing something about them is what tuning is all about.

This book will help you set up your boat for maximum speed, and show you how to modify the rig and sail controls to keep going fast in all windstrengths. It aims to demystify the black art of tuning, and show that rigs behave in a logical, predictable way. It also takes a hard look at trimming, because it's the trimmer's hard work that inches the boat to the front of the fleet.

Most rig tuning is aimed at speed to windward, so the bulk of this book covers beating. Later chapters look at ways of increasing offwind speed, although the finer points of mast bend and position are not so relevant once the kite is up.

There is a huge variation in rig designs, so I have concentrated on the three that are most common: masthead, fractional (with runners) and fractional (without runners). Between them, these configurations illustrate all the basic principles and by studying them carefully you should be able to set up your own boat whatever its rig. Now over to you – and good speed!

Lawrie Smith

Assembling the gear

Careful tuning can do a lot to improve the performance of an existing rig, but for best results the process should start right back at the design stage.

One-design boats

When you are trying to get to the top of any class it is essential to use proven equipment. Once you are on level terms with the best around you can afford to experiment with your own ideas, but until then it is best to copy the experts.

If you can't identify the best equipment because the top people all seem to have different ideas, then spend time talking to them and find out why they use what they do. This will give you a sound basis for a decision, and is better than following your own intuition.

Explain your plans to your sailmaker and ask him what he can do to help you. He should be able to give you measurements of spreader length and angle, mast rake and shroud tension, derived from successful boats that are using his sails. If he can't supply these figures immediately, ask him to find out what they are. If he seems unwilling, change your sailmaker.

A good sailmaker is vital. He must be willing and able to help you set up the boat. He must also be able to repeat your sails should you wish to order another set prior to your championships. It is no good spending months tuning your boat around your sails, achieving good speed, only to find out that your sails have stretched out of shape and you can't repeat them in new materials. The sailmaker must have a system of making sails from a template or a computer program; he must also have a system of testing the sailcloth because the cloth is just as important as the cut of the sail.

All too often sailmakers change their ideas and find they are unable to go back to previous designs, having either lost their cut sheets or discovered that a particular batch of cloth is no longer available. All these things must be assessed or you could easily end up wasting a lot of money.

Below: The spreader angle is logged as the distance between the mast and a line stretched between the spreader tips.

If your sailmaker can't give you the champion's rig settings, you may be able to measure his boat for yourself and then copy his system:

• Check the *mast rake* by measuring his forestay length, or by hoisting a tape measure on the main halyard and measuring the distance from the top of the mast to the top centre of the transom.

• Measure the *spreader length*.

• Measure the *spreader angle* by laying a straight edge between the tips of the spreaders and noting the distance from the mast to the straight edge.

• Measure the *rig tension* by using a tensiometer on the lowers and uppers (this is accurate to about 10lbs).

• Measure the *pre-bend* by tensioning the main halyard between the mast tip and the gooseneck and noting the distance between mast and halyard at the mid-point.

• Measure the mast step position using a tape measure laid from the mast to the transom.

Below: Pre-bend is logged as the distance between the mast and a line stretched from masthead to gooseneck.

Below: Measure the mast step position by logging the distance from the back of the mast to the transom.

One-off boats.

Deciding on the builder, designer, mastmaker and sailmaker for a new 'one-off' boat is always a tricky task. Cost is obviously important and often the deciding factor, but a number of considerations should be borne in mind:

Designer
● Previous boats: how successful have they been?
● How does the proposed design differ from his previous boat, and why has he made the alterations?
● What level of commitment can the design office offer? How many hours are they prepared to spend on the boat once she has been built?
● How far will the boatbuilder co-operate in making sure the boat is actually built to the designed lines and weights on the drawing?

Boatbuilder
● Does the builder have much experience of this size of boat and method of construction?
● Can he guarantee a delivery date?
● Can he offer a commitment to carry out any modifications or repairs once the boat is sailing?

Sail and spar maker
● Which boats are using their equipment? How do they rate?
● What is the proposed inventory?
● How much time are they prepared to set aside to sail on and tune the boat?
● Will repeat sails in the same cloth be available?
   No matter what type of design you eventually decide upon you must be aware of the time needed to work a boat up to its full potential. You should allow at least three months from the launch date to the championship itself.

Definitions

Twist   The change in the leech angle to the wind as sighted from behind looking from bottom to top.

Fullness or depth   The amount of 'belly' or 'sag' in the sail measured as the distance between the curved sail and an imaginary straight-edge laid between the luff and the leech.

Position of flow or maximum depth   The position of maximum depth is measured at a given height, for example: at mid stripe 50% aft. This means that at the mid-point between the head and the tack, the sail has its maximum fullness halfway between the luff and the leech.

Round or fine entry   A round or fine entry describes the curvature in the sail's leading edge.

Round or straight exit   This describes the curvature in the last 30% of the sail (the sail's leech area).

Weather helm   A boat with weather helm wants to point up into the wind when you let go of the tiller.

Lee helm   Reverse of weather helm.

Neutral helm   The boat wants to go in a straight line.

Telltales   These are short trips of wool or fabric stuck to the sail to indicate the airflow across it.

Centre of lateral resistance   The centre of lateral resistance or centre of effort is the point at which the rig is positioned relative to the hull to make the boat 'balance'.

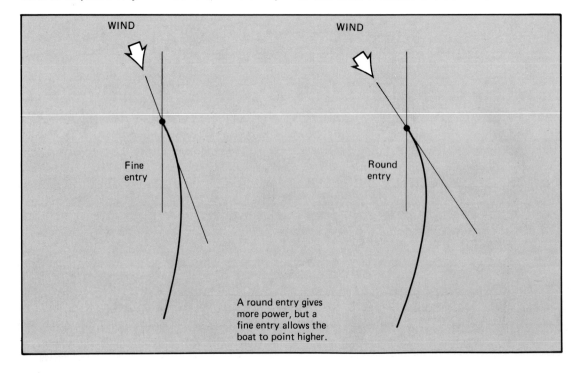

WIND   WIND

Fine entry

Round entry

A round entry gives more power, but a fine entry allows the boat to point higher.

Balancing the boat

A perfectly balanced boat will sail to windward on its own in a straight line. Moving the centre of lateral resistance aft by moving the rig aft will turn the boat into the wind producing weather helm, while moving it forward will result in lee helm.

Always aim to sail to windward with a small amount of weather helm, so when the helm is let go the boat slowly turns into the wind. Neutral or lee helm are both disastrous as 'lift' off the rudder is lost. Ideally you should have between two and five degrees of helm (measured as rudder angle off the centreline). Any more than five degrees will result in excessive drag from the steeply angled rudder.

Ways of changing the balance

Mast rake Raking the mast aft moves the total force on the sails further aft and increases weather helm. Raking the mast forward does the reverse.

Inshore, you are able to alter the rake before the race to suit the conditions on the day. Offshore, tune for medium winds unless you can guarantee the windstrength.

Mast heel position Move the heel of the mast aft to increase weather helm (and vice versa).

Genoa tack position Moving the genoa tack aft will increase weather helm (and vice versa).

Sail selection Different combinations of sails will affect balance. A full main with a number two genoa will give more weather helm than a reefed main with the same genoa.

Sail shape Full, tight-leeched sails will generate more weather helm than flat open-leeched sails.

Mainsheet traveller Pulling the traveller to weather will increase weather helm (and vice versa).

Crew position Moving crew members to weather will decrease heel and reduce weather helm (and vice versa).

Keel position Moving the keel forward increases weather helm (and vice versa).

Normally you will tune for medium winds. In lighter airs this can lead to lee helm because the boat heels less. Cure this by pulling the traveller to weather (powering up the main) and by moving crew weight to leeward. In strong winds the boat heels more so drop the traveller down and pile the crew on the weather rail. You are aiming for a constant two to five degrees of helm.

Left: Even a really big yacht can have its balance improved by piling the crew on the weather rail.

Tuning the rig

There are three types of rig in common use on keelboats and yachts: masthead rigs, fractional rigs with runners, and fractional rigs with swept-back spreaders and no runners. The tuning process is much the same for all three but because the elements of each rig have different functions the actual adjustments may differ from rig to rig.

When using the tuning system which follows, bear these differences in mind. If the headstay tension needs increasing, for example, the method of achieving this varies but the result will be the same: a finer genoa luff entry.

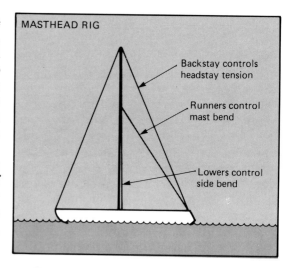

MASTHEAD RIG

Backstay controls headstay tension

Runners control mast bend

Lowers control side bend

*Right: The three main types of rig –
masthead, fractional with runners (centre)
and fractional with swept-back spreaders
and no runners (far right).*

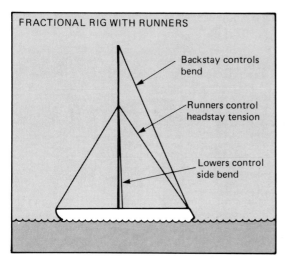

FRACTIONAL RIG WITH RUNNERS

Backstay controls bend

Runners control headstay tension

Lowers control side bend

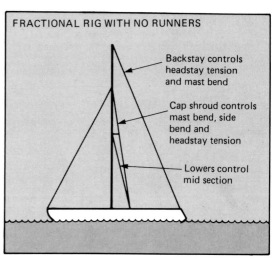

FRACTIONAL RIG WITH NO RUNNERS

Backstay controls headstay tension and mast bend

Cap shroud controls mast bend, side bend and headstay tension

Lowers control mid section

Fore-and-aft bend

The fore-and-aft bend of the mast can be set up by careful adjustment of the headstay, backstay shrouds and spreaders, and the runners and babystay if fitted.

Headstay
The length of your headstay determines upwind mast rake. The longer you make it the further aft your mast will rake and vice versa. Increasing tension in the headstay will reduce genoa luff sag, creating a finer entry in the sail. Reducing headstay tension will do the reverse.

Backstay – masthead rig
On a masthead-rigged boat the backstay controls headstay tension, mast bend and offwind mast rake.

Increasing backstay tension will increase headstay tension and also bend the mast by compression. Easing the backstay will allow the mast to rake forward when sailing downwind.

Backstay – fractional rig with runners
On this rig the backstay controls mast bend, mainly at the tip of the mast. Applying tension to a very flexible topmast will affect the tip only, but tension applied to a stiff mast will affect the whole spar.

Backstay – fractional rig without runners
In this case the backstay controls headstay tension and mast bend. The stiffer the topmast the tighter you can make the forestay without inducing excessive mast bend.

Above: On a fractional boat, applying backstay tension bends the mast and opens the leech of the mainsail.

Runners and checkstays – masthead rig

On a masthead rig the runners and checkstays simply control fore-and-aft bend. Increasing their tension reduces mast bend; reducing their tension increases it. They must however be adjusted in conjunction with the backstay, which also affects mast bend: easing the backstay without easing the runners will straighten the mast and vice versa. Remember that increasing the backstay tension without increasing tension in the runners could result in excessive compression forces breaking the mast.

Runners and checkstays – fractional rig

On a fractional-rig boat the runners control headstay tension while the checkstays control fore-and-aft bend.

Above: Reducing backstay tension lets the mast straighten up, which closes the mainsail leech.

Above: The checkstays are joined to the mast at mid-height, and attached to the runners at their lower ends.

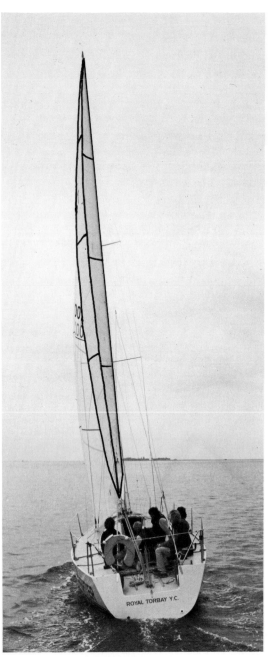

Left: Letting off the checkstays (far left) allows the mast to bend more, depowering the main. With the checkstays on the sail is fuller (near left).

Babystay

The babystay is a useful and often essential stay which controls fore-and-aft bend.

Increasing the tension on the babystay when going to windward will bend the mast, particularly low down. Downwind it should be in tension to keep the mast in column: it will be working directly against the thrust of the spinnaker pole, preventing the mast from inverting. The stay should also be tensioned when going to windward in heavy airs or rough water to reduce the chance of inversion.

Pre-bend

This is the amount of bend set into the mast before the mainsail is hoisted or the backstay tensioned. Pre-bend can be achieved in a number of ways:

● By angling the spreaders aft of a straight line between the masthead and the shroud plates – as the shrouds are tensioned the spreaders force the middle of the mast forward.

● By adding chocks behind the mast at deck level, thus simply forcing bend into it.

● By setting up a compression force between the shrouds and the headstay. The shroud plates must be behind the mast if this is to work.

● Through tension in the lower shrouds. The lower shroud plates must be forward of the mast for this to work.

Side bend controls

Fore-and-aft bend is an essential element of sail control, but side bend has to be eradicated. This is the job of the shrouds and spreaders.

Spreaders

Increasing the length of your spreaders will increase the sideways stiffness of the mast providing the shroud tension remains constant, and vice versa.

Shrouds

Increasing the tension in the shrouds will increase the sideways stiffness of the mast providing the spreaders force the shrouds out of a straight line – that is outboard of the line that they would take if there were no spreaders. Despite this you should fit the shortest spreaders possible by tuning them in conjunction with shroud tension. If you have maximum shroud tension and your mast is bending sideways going to weather, then your spreaders are too short. If your mast stays straight using very little tension the spreaders could be shorter.

Lower shrouds

The lower shrouds are there to support the mast sideways and also to hold it in column, preventing it from 'popping' to leeward or windward when going upwind. They also work directly against the thrust from the spinnaker pole and jockey pole when beam reaching.

Increasing their tension will stiffen the mast at lower spreader level both sideways and fore-and-aft. But take care: excessive tension will result in the lower shrouds taking over from the main shrouds, and the mast will fall over above the lower spreaders. Too little tension will result in the mast dipping to leeward through the force of the windward lower spreader.

Stepping the mast

Having seen what everything does, it's time to step the mast and set up the rig. When it's roughly right, you can go sailing and do the fine tuning.

Checking the mast fittings

Lay the mast along a bench and make sure the heel tenon is dead central and a perfect fit. If the tenon can move the mast will twist and your spreader settings will become haphazard. Working up the mast, check that the gooseneck is central and make sure it is in the correct position relative to the black band. Check that the spreader bracket is strong and will not deflect under load – even one millimetre of deflection will make your spreader settings useless. Make sure the bracket is central by measuring from each tip to the luff groove in the mast.

Check that the shrouds connect into the mast at the correct position according to class rules – in most classes this will be as high as possible. The spinnaker halyard should be as high as class rules permit. At the tip of the mast the black band must be as high as possible and the main halyard should hoist the mainsail right up so that the top of the sail is level with the lower edge of the band. Any section of the spar above this point is unnecessary windage, just where it hurts performance most.

Below: Align the gooseneck with the track by sighting along the mast.

Below: Ensure the spreader brackets are symmetrical by measuring to the track.

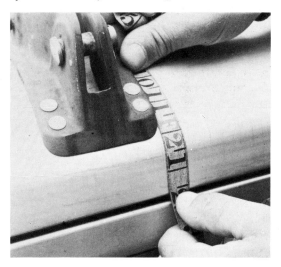

Putting it all together

Once you are happy that your mast and rigging are in order step the mast into the boat. Attach the headstay and backstay and adjust their lengths until the mast is raked five degrees aft of vertical. Check this by running a plumb line to the masthead and measuring its distance behind the mast; alternatively get off the boat and sight the mast side-on, using the horizon as a datum.

Run the end of a long tape measure up on the main halyard and measure the distance from the masthead to a fixed point on the transom to give yourself a starting reference for setting up the rake.

Make sure that the mast is a tight fit in both the partners and the mast step. If the mast is allowed to twist the spreader settings will be upset. If the mast moves sideways at deck level there is also a chance of unwanted sidebend low down.

Connect the shrouds onto their chainplates and take up the tension on both shrouds, counting the number of turns on each bottlescrew (turnbuckle). Apply as much tension as possible; the final turns will have to go on while the boat is sailing to windward.

Connect the lower shrouds and tension

Left and below: Stretch a long tape measure from the masthead to the transom to measure the mast rake.

them in the same way and to the same degree as the shrouds, remembering that fewer turns will be required to achieve the same tension as there is less stretch in a shorter length of rod or wire. (When the rig is fully tuned you will probably find that the lower shrouds are tighter. But for the time being set them to the same tension).

Check the distance between the front of the mast and the forward edge of the mast partners. Use quarter-inch chocks to fill the gap so that on your first sail the mast will set up fairly straight.

Below: Measure from the masthead to each chainplate to check that the mast is vertical across the boat.

Setting the spreaders

The mast is now in the boat with headstay, backstay and shrouds connected. Your spreaders are the same length but they are probably not at the same height at their outboard ends, nor are they at the same fore-and-aft angle.

The spreaders can be adjusted ashore. First send someone aloft to measure from the hounds down to each spreader tip so that they can be seized off at equal heights.

Next, run light strings from the hounds to the chainplates and measure the distance between the spreader and the string on each side. If there is a discrepancy then adjust by either twisting the mast at step level – by moving the mast heel or the mast tenon – or adjusting one of the spreaders so that it matches. If you have a double or triple spreader rig you must assume that the spreaders are aligned with each other, and adjust by twisting the mast.

You now have the entire rig symmetrical and are ready to go sailing. Remember however that any further adjustment on a port shroud or spreader must be matched on starboard or the whole process will have to be repeated.

Setting up the mast

The ideal windspeed for a trial sail is 12-15 knots. Until you have the mast properly set up, hoist mainsail only.

Steer the boat onto a close reach and tighten the leeward shroud, taking up half the slack. Count the number of turns you have taken and repeat the exercise on the lower shroud. Tack over and repeat on the opposite shrouds.

Side bend

Put the boat hard on the wind and go through the same procedure until the leeward shroud is just taut. Keeping the boat on the wind, sight up the mast and study the side bend. What you are looking for is a perfectly straight spar on both tacks. If the topmast is falling over to leeward on both tacks then either the shrouds are too slack, the spreaders are too short or the lower shrouds are too tight.

When the lowers are too tight they 'load up' before the shrouds and the mast simply leans over above them. If the shrouds are too slack the mast will fall over to leeward owing to lack of tension. The first step is to tighten the shrouds until you feel any more tension will be extreme. If this does not cure the problem then gradually ease off on the lowers one turn at a time. As you do this, check that the middle section of the mast at lower spreader level isn't bowing to leeward. If it is then you must return the lowers to their original tension as the problem must be that the shrouds are stretching or the upper spreaders are too short.

If you have shroud stretch your shroud size is just too small and the wire or rod is stretching under load. Check out other boats of your size and if your rigging is suspect then change it for a thicker gauge.

If your upper spreaders are too short they will give insufficient support to the mast section above the lower spreaders. Again look at other boats. As a rule each upper spreader should force the shroud out of line by at least three inches.

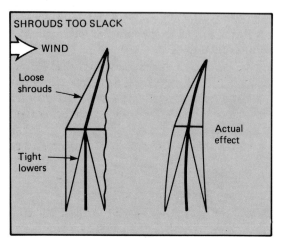

SHROUDS TOO SLACK
WIND
Loose shrouds
Actual effect
Tight lowers

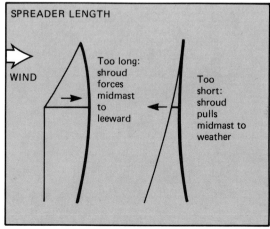

SPREADER LENGTH
WIND
Too long: shroud forces midmast to leeward
Too short: shroud pulls midmast to weather

If you find that the mast is straight on one tack but not the other then you have a discrepancy in either your rod/wire lengths or the height of your chainplates.

Problem 1   The mast falls over to leeward on one tack but not on the other.

Answer   Ease off the shroud on the 'straight' tack and tighten by the same number of turns on the opposite tack until the mast is either straight or bends to the same degree on both tacks.

Problem 2   The mast dips to leeward at spreader level on one tack but not the other.

Answer   As before, but ease and tighten the lowers.

Fore-and-aft bend

Once you are happy that sidebend is zero on both tacks, sight up the mast and check that fore-and-aft bend is equal on both tacks. To do this accurately you must mark your mainsail at mid-luff height with coloured lines drawn at one-inch intervals from three inches aft of the luff rope to 18 inches aft. You can then set up a taut string from masthead to gooseneck which will cross the marks on the mainsail. This will show you exactly how much bend you are carrying. On *Victory 83* we had two lines permanently set up for checking bend in various wind strengths and checking that the bend was equal on both tacks. Mast bend can also be worked out from side-on photographs by laying a ruler along the photo from mast head to gooseneck. By counting the number of marks between mast and ruler your exact bend measurement can be established.

If you find that fore-and-aft bend is different on each tack, then either your spreader angles are out, or your runners or checks are different lengths. To ensure that they are the same go ashore and bring them up to the same tension; before releasing, mark each one with a marker pen so that they can then be set up identically when sailing.

Left: As you tighten the shrouds, sight up the mast to check for side bend (inset).

Tuning the genoa

Before you hoist a genoa you need to mark off your tiller or wheel so that you can see exactly how much helm you are using to keep the boat on course.

If you have a tiller, mark off one-degree quadrants under the tiller with a marker pen. If your boat has a wheel attach a piece of tape at the top of the wheel when the rudder is central. Then when the wheel is over with the tape at, say, quarter past, you can work out how much helm you are using.

Having hoisted the genoa your first objective is to check out the balance of the boat. With full main and No.1 genoa in medium air you should have between two and five degrees of weather helm. If, with the crew all up to weather and the sails set approximately right, you are finding the balance all wrong, then return to shore and adjust the mast rake. Rake it aft if you have neutral or lee helm, and forward if you have weather helm. Once you are happy that the balance of the boat is about right, settle with the rake you have and begin tuning the sails because they alone can affect the balance quite considerably.

To get the best performance from the sail the following controls must be constantly adjusted as the wind and sea conditions change:

- Backstay tension (masthead rig)
- Runner tension (fractional rig)
- Halyard tension
- Car position
- Sheet tension

Backstay tension – masthead rig

In a masthead rig the backstay controls the tension in the headstay. A slack backstay gives a slack headstay which in turn sags aft and to leeward creating a full sail with a 'round' entry. A tight backstay does the reverse, flattening the sail and producing a fine entry. The backstay tension can therefore drastically change the characteristics of a genoa.

However, increasing and decreasing the tension also alters the mast bend. You must therefore have an understanding of how to use this control in conjunction with the runners, checkstays and mast chocks so that correct mast bend can also be achieved in all conditions.

Runner tension – fractional rig

On a fractional rig the runners control the headstay tension, since they lead to the same part of the mast.

If no runners are fitted then some headstay tension can be achieved by tensioning the backstay, though this will inevitably bend the mast.

How much tension?

With the telltales positioned at one-third, half and two-thirds height, and nine inches behind the luff, sail the boat to windward with the genoa cars in their middle position – that is where an extension of the genoa sheet would bisect the clew and hit the luff at mid height. Tension the genoa halyard so that the horizontal creases appearing out of the luff just disappear. Sheet the sail so that all three telltales are lifting together and note the fullness and position of maximum depth in the sail.

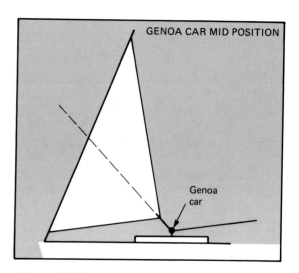

Above: With the car in its mid-position an extension of the genoa sheet would meet the luff at its mid-point.

Keeping the boat hard on the wind, increase the backstay tension (masthead rig) or runners (fractional rig). This will fine the entry of the sail and enable you to point higher.

There will come a point where the entry becomes too fine and to maintain speed you will find yourself sailing with the windward telltales flowing all the time. If you have no speedo or cannot judge speed then check your heel angle, which will drop if you point so high that the weather telltales begin to break. As you should never sail the boat in medium airs with anything less than maximum power, you will know that the entry must be too fine. At this point you have overcooked the backstay (or runners) and you should gradually ease it off until the weather telltales are just breaking.

When the breeze drops headstay sag will be reduced, so the backstay or runners will have to be eased to keep the luff of the sail at a constant depth, and if necessary to increase the fullness even further to make the sail fuller for the lighter air.

In a building breeze more tension will be required to achieve the opposite.

Above: Headstay tension is controlled by the runners on a fractional rig, and by the backstay on a masthead rig. On this fractional boat slack runners result in headstay sag and make the genoa entry full (left). Tightening the runners straightens the headstay, making the genoa flatter and giving a finer entry (above).

Halyard tension

As you apply tension to the genoa halyard you will move the draft in the sail further forward. The softer or stretchier the cloth, the larger the adjustment will need to be. A 12-metre's heavy Kevlar genoa requires only four inches of travel, whereas a standard Dacron sail will need up to 18 inches.

Leaving the halyard in one position for all wind strengths would result in the 'flow' being too far forward in light airs and too far aft in a breeze.

Experience and experimentation are essential if a genoa trimmer is to learn how to achieve the correct position of flow simply by looking at a sail, but the basic rule is to keep the flow aft in light airs and forward in a breeze. Increasing the halyard tension holds or moves the flow forward, while easing the halyard tension does the reverse.

Right: Excessive genoa halyard tension drags the draft too far forward.

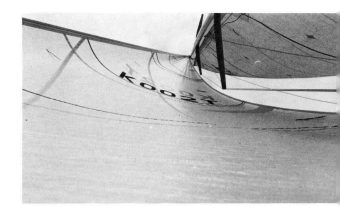

Right: If the halyard is too loose the draft is too far aft.

Right: With the halyard properly adjusted the draft position is ideal.

Genoa car position and sheet tension

Moving the car forward increases the depth of the sail, and vice versa. Moving the car inboard closes the slot and decreases the sail's angle of attack to the wind, and vice versa.

As the car is moved forward the sheet must also be eased in order to keep all three telltales breaking together. But by easing the sheet the slot becomes wider, which is wrong because you will have moved the car forward to generate more power. You must therefore also bring the car inboard to maintain slot width. In some cases it may be appropriate to bring it inboard still further to decrease the slot width. In short, as the car goes forward it should come inboard.

Below: Check the shape and angle of the genoa by sighting from the leeward rail.

Above: An efficient system for moving the genoa car is vital for good sail setting.

Right: Moving the genoa car too far aft flattens the sail.

Right: With the car too far forward the sail is too full.

Right: Adjust the car position and sheet tension to achieve the most efficient sail shape.

Above: With the genoa car pulled outboard the slot is too wide for the conditions.

Above: Move the genoa car inboard to close the slot and generate more power from the rig.

Above: With the genoa car hauled right in, the slot is the correct width for this wind strength.

As the breeze increases you must initially move the car onto the outboard track, and then begin sliding it aft. As the car is moved back, increase sheet tension, again to keep all three telltales breaking together.

Above: The genoa sheet must be adjusted with the car. Here it is too loose.

Above: When the sheet is too tight the slot at the top of the sail is far too small.

Above: The right sheet tension maintains the correct slot width and sail depth.

Medium-air beating

In medium airs of 10-15 knots full main and No.1 genoa must be set unless your particular class of boat is very tender, for maximum power is required from the rig. With a masthead boat most of the drive is developed from the genoa, and it is crucial for the sail to be set correctly. Your sailmaker will have cut the sail with a given depth and position of flow at one-third, half and two-thirds height. It is your job to set the sail to these figures, changing them only when the sail has to act either below or above its designed wind range. Examples of such figures are given below.

The best way to check that your setting corresponds to the sailmaker's figures is to take photos as shown and work out the draft and position. Note that draft stripes are essential for accurate setting.

Imagine the sail to be a critical aircraft wing and treat it as such. If the sail has too much halyard the draft will be too far forward. If the headstay tension is excessive the draft will be too far aft, resulting in an overflat sail. Oversheeting will flatten the sail, close the head and backwind the mainsail. Undersheeting will make the sail too full and open the leech, and pointing will suffer.

	Maximum draft	Draft position
Lower speed stripe	10%	38% aft
Middle speed stripe	12%	42% aft
Top speed stripe	14%	45% aft

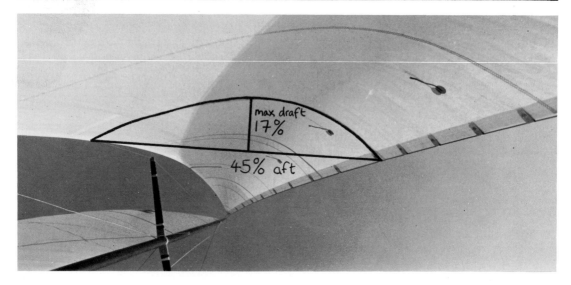

Above: Work out the depth and draft position by drawing on a photograph.

Going to windward in a small chop

Sheet the sail with all three telltales lifting together, giving the sail an even angle of attack. If this backwinds the mainsail move the car aft and try again. This first step will flatten the genoa and reduce the amount of air being thrown back into the mainsail. With the mainsail traveller on centreline you should just see the luff of the sail lifting. If there is no sign of backwind then the slot is too open, or if the sail is lifting all the way back to the battens, the slot is too closed. Adjust the car position until you have the right amount of backwind; sheet tension will be governed by the alignment of the telltales.

Twist

When deciding on how much twist to set into the sail you have to consider the wind sheer, wind strength and sea state.

Wind sheer

In Newport, sailing the twelves, we were finding big changes in wind direction between the deck and the masthead. Usually, we were having to sail with more twist on starboard tack than on port. You will obviously not have such a big problem unless your boat has an 80-foot mast. Nevertheless wind sheer must be detected before the start of any race.

To check for sheer, position the boat head to wind by lying the main boom along the centreline of the boat. Look up the mast and decide if the wind indicator is also lying along the centreline. If not, then set your sails with more twist on starboard tack if the burgee is pointing to starboard, and vice versa. On the opposite tack you will have to sail with zero twist, and you may still find difficulty in getting your top telltales to flow properly; you will almost certainly achieve better boat speeds and angles on the tack with twist set in the sail. If you have an electronic wind indicator then note your compass heading whilst head to wind and then note your wind direction reading. If, say, your compass reads 100 degrees and your wind direction reads 110 degrees you know that you have a ten-degree veer with height. Your genoa trimmer will also get a good feel for the wind if he trims initially on both tacks. He will find he has to trim harder on one tack, and set his cars in different positions.

Wind strengths and sea state

The basic rules for wind strength and sea state are as follows:

- Rough water: full sails, with twist.
- Flat water: flat sails, less twist.
- Heavy airs: flat sails, with twist.
- Medium airs: full sails, less twist.
- Light airs: Medium-to-full sails depending on the boat, with twist.

Rough water In rough sea conditions you will need all the power you can get from the genoa to punch you through the waves. Set the car on the inboard track, positioned well forward. You won't be able to point very high without a big loss of speed, so the sail will have to be well eased. Depending on wind sheer, set the twist in the sail by looking at the telltales. But if you have to set the leech with excessive twist to get the telltales to flow, then ignore them as the slot will be too wide and power will be lost. If the mainsail backwinds with all three telltales flowing, then ease the sheet instead of moving the car aft. This can pay, because you retain the power in the lower two-thirds of the sail for a small sacrifice in the head.

Flat water Because there are no waves, the boat will accelerate and stay at speed fairly easily. You can therefore point closer to the wind, and you must adapt your sails accordingly. Move the car further aft than for rough seas, and sheet the sail so that the foot is almost bar tight or right up against the rigging at its base. In most classes you will also be able to sheet the sail right onto the spreader tips. The only twist you will need will be for wind sheer, but if you find other boats going faster but lower than yourselves some twist may be useful. Twist equals speed but poor pointing. If you need to foot fast for tactical reasons, then simply ease the sheet a fraction to open the slot and gain speed.

Heavy airs Set the car on the outboard track well aft to keep the slot wide with plenty of twist. Increase the halyard tension to drag the flow forward, which in turn will also open up the head of the sail. You should also have maximum backstay tension on a masthead rig, or maximum runner tension on a fractional rig. This will ensure that the headstay is as straight as possible.

Sheet the sail so that the foot is bar tight and the head is twisting open. A small amount of backwind is acceptable, but if the mainsail gets out of control move the car further aft and don't worry if the top telltale is breaking before the lower telltales.

Light airs In these conditions you need maximum drive from the sail but you must make sure that the weak airflow can make its way across the sail without stalling. Set the car on the inboard track, a little further aft than for medium airs. You will need more twist in these conditions to open the slot so that the air doesn't have to fight its way through a narrow escape route. Ease the halyard until you see small creases forming out of the luff and ease the backstay until you have an angle of attack that the helmsman can sail to.

Because there is a small load in the sail, headstay sag will be minimal and probably less than the sail is cut for, so you may have to ease the backstay or runners (depending on the rig) right off to achieve a round enough entry.

Playing the genoa in gusts

Having set the sail up before the start you have arrived at reasonable settings for the car, halyard, backstay and runners. The next problem is to adjust these controls for varying wind and wave patterns or for tactical reasons.

Typical boat conversation

HELMSMAN: Going nicely now, the boat feels good – how's the genoa look?

GENOA TRIMMER: Looks OK, but do you feel like trimming it in a little? We still have plenty of twist up top and the speed's still on the high side.

HELMSMAN: OK, let's try that. Bring it in a touch, but keep an eye on the speedo.

MAINSAIL TRIMMER: If you're going to do that, hang on a second. My mainsail is lifting just right and I'll need to bend the mast a little to flatten it off.

The genoa is sheeted in three inches, the mast bent one inch more and speed drops by 0.1 knots. The apparent wind goes from 30 degrees to 27 degrees so they have made a gain.

HELMSMAN: There are some nasty waves approaching; watch the speed and get ready to crack the sheets a little.

The genoa trimmer eases the sheet and moves the car forward to maintain twist and angle of attack. Simply easing the sheet will open the head too much and power and pointing will suffer. The backstay (runners on a fractional rig) is also eased to round up the entry and give the sail a touch more depth. The helmsman steers a couple of degrees lower and maintains speed through the chop.

HELMSMAN: OK, the speed's building fast, bring her back in again. In fact we're now going a little too fast for our optimum V.M.G. and I feel I can go higher still. The water is getting smoother as we close on this shore.

The genoa trimmer tightens the backstay (runners on a fractional rig), moves the car onto the inboard track and slides it further aft to flatten the sail for the smoother water. The sheet is pulled in harder to maintain twist. The genoa trimmer must now work in close liaison with the helmsman, easing the sheet and moving the car forward to build speed and doing the reverse to gain height.

The windspeed increases by five knots.

MAINSAIL TRIMMER: I'm beginning to get too much backwind and I have maximum mast bend and flattener.

The genoa trimmer increases the backstay tension (with a fractional rig the runner man tensions the runner) to straighten the headstay. This compensates for the extra headstay sag caused by the increase in apparent wind speed. He increases the halyard tension to drag the flow forward and moves the car further aft on the outboard track. He then sheets the sail harder to keep the top of the sail working.

GENOA TRIMMER: How's that?

MAINSAIL TRIMMER: Better, but I'm· still getting too much backwind.

The genoa trimmer applys maximum backstay (runner on a fractional rig) and halyard, moves the car further aft still and sheets in a little harder. The top telltale is breaking before the middle one, which is breaking before the bottom one,

GENOA TRIMMER: If the breeze builds any more we'll have to go to the No. 2...

Setting the No. 2 genoa

Assume you have your No. 1 heavy genoa set. The wind speed has risen to 20 knots true and you must decide if it will pay to go to a smaller sail.

Your decision should be based on the following:

The distance left to the mark If you are only five minutes from the mark, a change will cost you more than you gain from having a faster sail. In boats of less than 45 feet, having a man on the bow reduces speed dramatically, to say nothing of the interference caused by the actual change.

Conditions ahead Anticipate the effect on the apparent wind as you sail into a stronger or weaker tidal flow. An increase in the tide under you, for example, will increase the apparent wind. Consider any tactics that you may have to employ further up the course. Frequent tacking (up a shoreline for instance) will result in a drop in average boat speed and subsequent apparent wind speed. Will the first reach be broad enough to carry a spinnaker? If not, you will need your No. 1 genoa and holding onto it now could pay big dividends down the reach.

But if you have decided to set the No. 2, you must now quickly adjust your settings to get back into top gear.

Backstay/runner

A No. 2 will be cut with more hollow in the luff than a No. 1, so a reduction in backstay tension (runner tension on a fractional rig) may be necessary to get the correct angle of attack. The wind has much more force in it now, so a finer entry will be needed to cope with it. Sail the boat as with the No. 1, setting the sail initially around the telltales.

Halyard

Use plenty of halyard to keep the flow in its designed position, which in any case will be well forward.

Genoa car

Because the No. 2 will be shorter along the foot, the sail's sheeting angle will automatically be wider if you stay on the track used for the No. 1 – but as you need a wider slot for this sail it is sensible to simply slide the car forward using the same track.

Set the sail applying the principles used for the No. 1, but do not twist the head off until the wind speed increases so much that you are having trouble with backwind.

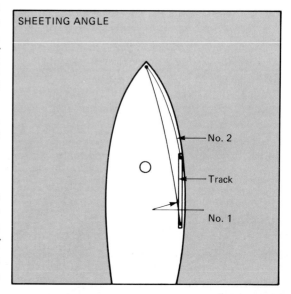

SHEETING ANGLE

No. 2

Track

No. 1

Setting the No. 3 jib

The No. 3 should be set before any reefs are put into the mainsail. Ideally the sail should be cut so that the clew is roughly six inches above the deck at shroud position. No overlap is required, so the mainsheet traveller can be dropped down to leeward without any risk of backwinding.

Because the sail has such a high aspect ratio, your sheet angle must be more vertical to keep the head under control. The flow should be designed to be well forward in the sail so excessive halyard won't be required. If the boat is overpowered with this sail set, then try easing the sheet a little to get the air moving off the sail more easily. If this destroys pointing ability it could well pay to sheet it back in and reef the main.

Car position

The jib track should be set further inboard than the No. 1 and No. 2 track. It usually pays to have one track just inside the shroud base and one just outside. Moving them further outboard will create an angle of attack that is too wide for the sail. Backwinding shouldn't be a problem so there is no reason to open the slot any further. Use the outboard track only in extreme conditions.

Tuning the mainsail

As with headsails the shape of the mainsail is determined by the interaction of a number of sail controls.

Backstay, runners, checks and mast chocks – masthead rigs
Increasing backstay tension will increase bend, flatten the mainsail and move the flow in the sail further aft.

An increase in backstay tension must be matched with an increase in the tension on runners and checks, and vice versa. The 'chocks' or deck ram must be adjustble to control the bend in the lower section of the spar. Adding chocks in front of the mast create a stiffer section, producing a fuller, more powerful mainsail.

Backstay, runners, checks and mast chocks – fractional rigs
Increasing runner tension will increase bend (through compression), flatten the mainsail and move the flow in the sail further aft. The increase must be matched

Above: If the mainsheet is too loose the leech will be too open (with the top telltale flying).

Above: Too much tension closes the leech (shown by the top telltale collapsing).

Above: When the top leech telltale is on the break the mainsheet tension is correct.

by an adjustment in the checks. The chocks may also need adjusting to maintain the bend in the lower part of the mast.

An increase in runner tension will slacken the backstay and therefore tighten the mainsail leech, so tension the backstay to maintain mainsail twist.

Sheet tension

Sheet tension controls leech tension. If the backstay is either slack or overridden by the mainsail, the mainsheet will also govern mast bend. More sheet tension will produce more bend, while easing the sheet allows the mast to straighten up.

Traveller
The traveller controls the mainsail's angle of attack to the wind, and the slot width. Bringing it to weather will open the slot and increase weather helm. Dropping it to leeward will do the reverse. Make sure that the traveller's track is curved so that sheet tension doesn't increase when it is dropped to leeward.

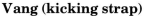

Vang (kicking strap)

When sailing upwind vang tension controls leech tension and mast bend – but only when it overrides the mainsheet. This can be useful when going to windward in heavy airs. Because of the angle at which the vang operates, it forces the mast forward at gooseneck level, bending the mast low down. This flattens the mainsail in its lower half and by doing so it also opens the slot. In light and medium airs the vang should be left slack to windward; use it for control of twist downwind.

Above: The traveller and mainsheet are played together to alter the shape of the main. Here, in light winds, the traveller is hauled to windward and the sheet eased to give a powerful sail shape (left). Lowering the traveller and hauling in the sheet gives a flatter sail which enables the boat to point higher (above). Note that the boom stays on the centreline unless the boat is overpowered.

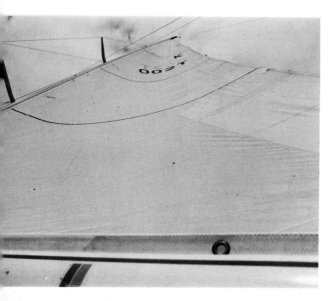

Cunningham and main halyard

Increasing the cunningham tension drags the flow forward in the sail. Because the mast is already bent, cunningham tension also increases bend by pulling down on the tip like the string of an archer's bow.

Adjusting the main halyard has the same effect, and it can be more advantageous if your mainsail is short of the black band at the top.

Battens

As a rule long battens, relative to mainsail width, should be tapered and short battens untapered. Using tapered battens where the batten length is almost half the sail width is fine because their inboard ends will follow the sail's camber. If the battens are shorter, their full length should be used to keep the exit of the sail straight. Choose soft battens for light airs and stiff ones for heavy airs.

Above: When the cunningham is pulled tight the draft in the sail is dragged forward (left). This is essential in strong winds. Easing the cunningham moves the draft back aft (above) which is more efficient in light winds.

Outhaul and flattener

The outhaul and flattener are used to control the depth of the base of the mainsail. Ideally your sail should be cut so that it is still out to its black band when the outhaul is eased for reaching. If not, you will be losing up to four inches of boom length when going downwind.

Instead of using the outhaul you can use the flatteners for controlling depth in the lower third of the sail without losing sail area. All you will lose is two to three inches of leech length, which is not as important when going to windward as boom length is when going downwind (see overleaf).

Above: The outhaul can be used to alter the depth at the the bottom of the main. If it is eased (left) the foot of the sail is too full for efficiency on the beat. Pulled too tight (centre) it flattens the sail out too much. When correctly adjusted (right) the bottom of the sail produces enough power without jeopardising pointing ability.

Above: Applying the flattener can be a more efficient way of reducing depth in the bottom of the main. Easing it off (right) gives more power.

Mainsail trim

You have the controls avilable to adjust:
- Amount of fullness
- Position of fullness
- Amount of twist
- Position of twist

Pull the cunningham on until the small horizontal creases forming out of the luff just disappear, and pull the outhaul or flattener on until a 'ridge' above the boom begins to form. Set the traveller so that the boom is on the centreline and tension the mainsheet until the top telltale on the leech – positioned one inch below the top batten – begins to break. Too much tension will stall the head of the sail and the telltale will lie down. Too little tension will make the head too open and the telltale will stream out straight. Study the draft

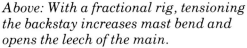

Above: With a fractional rig, tensioning the backstay increases mast bend and opens the leech of the main.

Above: Easing the backstay allows the mast to straighten up, giving a full sail and a tight leech.

stripes at one-third, half and two-thirds mast height very carefully.

Mast bend

Increasing mast bend will flatten the sail, move the flow aft and open the leech. Unfortunately as the wind increases you need to flatten the sail but you also need to bring the flow forward, not aft. Likewise as

the wind drops you need to increase the depth and move the flow aft, not forward. Obviously the best way of achieving this would be to change mainsails, using a flat sail with its flow well forward for strong winds and the opposite for light winds. Most classes however are allowed just the one sail, so a compromise sail shape must be used if it is to work in all conditions.

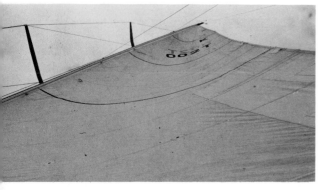

Above: With the mast too straight (top) the draft is too deep and too far forward. Excessive bend (centre) flattens the sail and brings the flow aft. In the bottom picture the sail shape is ideal.

Control over the position of flow is determined by:

- Cloth weight and stretch
- Luff tension
- Mast bend

As mentioned previously, more bend moves the flow aft, and less bend moves it forward. Increasing cunningham tension also moves the flow forward, the amount depending on the type of cloth. A stretchy cloth will enable you to change the shape of the sail more than a stable cloth which is fine except that the sail will also stretch down its leech and 'grow' bigger and therefore fuller as the breeze builds. It is more efficient to use a stable cloth which does not stretch so much, so that the sail will retain its shape – although its position of flow cannot be changed as easily.

The exception to this can be seen on the latest 'hi-tech' Kevlar-backed, Mylar-fronted sails, which combine the advantage of a stable leech with a flexible luff. For the majority of classes, however, Dacron is the norm; the sailor who understands the characteristics of his sail and uses that knowledge to the full will gain a significant advantage over his opponents.

What to look for

Having draft stripes on the sail is essential for assessing sail shape accurately. Without actually taking a camera on board and producing photographs as in this book, you will never know the exact figures. But with practice and experience you should be able to form a picture in your head of what the sail should look like in various wind strengths.

Visual aids: backwinding

An indication of the depth of the sail can be found by assessing the amount of backwinding. If there is no backwinding and your genoa is set on the inboard track with little twist, then almost certainly your mainsail is set too flat. If the genoa is open and the front 40 per cent of the mainsail is lifting then the mainsail is too full. As a start, with the genoa sheeted normally, adjust the bend so that you have approximately 20 per cent of the mainsail lifting.

Telltales

Having arrived at approximately the right amount of fullness you must now set the leech correctly. Position telltales below each batten pocket and apply enough mainsheet so that they are all flying, apart from the top one which should be on the verge of breaking. If they are not flying then the air is breaking off the sail before it reaches the leech.

Check that the traveller is not holding the boom above the centreline. Dropping the boom below the centreline will align the leech along the centreline of the boat, helping the telltales to fly. Pulling the boom above centre will 'hook' the leech to weather, promoting a stall. To start with, set the boom four inches below the centreline and if the telltales are still not flying check the mainsheet tension.

Right: If the traveller is holding the boom above the centreline the leech will hook to weather, stalling the airflow across the sail.

Easing the mainsheet will open the leech and make the telltales fly. It will also reduce pressure on the mast and decrease bend, resulting in a fuller sail. Pulling on the backstay will also free the leech but this time bend will increase and the sail will become flatter. Therefore work both the sheet and backstay (and runners too on a fractional rig) until you have a mainsail that is backwinding slightly with the lower telltales flowing. If the wind drops, ease the sheet and pull the traveller up to weather, bringing the boom onto the centreline. If it freshens, increase the sheet tension; if backwinding increases apply more backstay, all the time keeping the top telltale flowing.

Setting the base of the sail
The type of boat will determine just how full your sail should be in its base.

If you are sheeting the boom on the centreline, your sail must be reasonably 'flat' off the boom to prevent the lower leech from hooking and stalling. When sailing a boat with a very narrow sheeting angle, such as a 12-metre or a 6-metre, your slot will be narrow because the boat is narrow, and you must then keep the sail flat low down to prevent excessive backwinding. If you have a J24 your slot will be reasonably wide – because of class rules – and you will need a fuller sail low down to keep the slot width correct.

The basic rule are as follows:
● Narrow slot or sheeting angle: boom on centreline to open slot: flat mainsail low down to prevent hooking.
● Wide slot or sheeting angle: Boom below centreline to close slot: full mainsail low down to keep lower leech parallel with centreline.

The time to increase or decrease the depth of the base will depend on wind and sea conditions. If the sea is flat you will need to point high: the boom will have to be on or near the centreline and therefore the base must be flat to prevent 'hooking'. If you are experiencing a nasty left-over chop you will have the genoa eased for speed, allowing you to drop the traveller without increasing backwind. Dropping the boom below the centreline will enable you to ease the outhaul and power up the base, returning the lower batten to its parallel state.

Below: Adjusting the mainsail leech. Too open with too much twist (left), too tight (centre), and ideal (right).

Setting the top of the sail

There are two main factors to be taken into account when setting the upper third of the mainsail: wind sheer and wind speed.

Wind sheer If you have veer with height, you will need more twist on starboard tack. You must then sail with more fullness up top so that when the sheet is eased you will have enough drive from the top of the sail. On port tack you will need the reverse, sheeting harder to keep the telltale on the break and to flatten the upper third – so that the air doesn't stall by having to bend around too tight a curve.

Wind speed – masthead rig In light airs you require fullness with twist: this way you have the power from the sail combined with an open upper leech, which allows the weak air to escape before it stalls. Keep the backstay slack and ease the sheet, applying only enough backstay to maintain the correct headstay tension. As the wind rises increase the sheet tension, keeping the top telltale on the break, and increase the backstay tension to flatten the mainsail. If you require more headstay tension but no more bend (for choppy seas) then increase both the backstay and the runners/checks, so that the mast remains under control.

Wind speed – fractional rig As with the masthead rig, keep the backstay slack and ease the sheet to provide fullness with twist. Apply enough runner for correct headstay tension. As the wind builds increase the sheet tension and pull on the runners to keep the headstay sag under control.

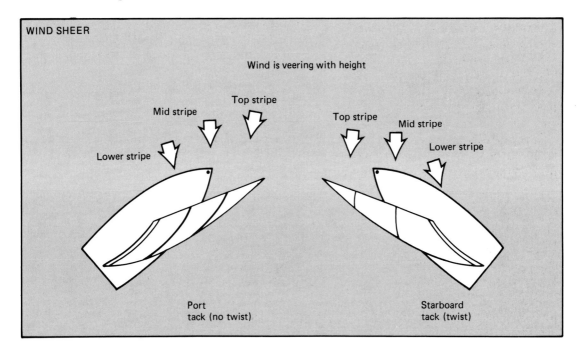

WIND SHEER

Wind is veering with height

Mid stripe · Top stripe · Lower stripe

Top stripe · Mid stripe · Lower stripe

Port tack (no twist)

Starboard tack (twist)

Setting the middle of the sail

The depth and position of flow in the middle of the sail is controlled by mast bend and cunningham tension.

Increasing the tension on the sheet or the backstay will increase bend and move the flow aft. To offset this you increase the cunningham tension whenever you increase the bend so that the flow moves forward, or at least holds position. In the strongest winds you must apply all the tension you can. The further forward you can move the draft in the sail, the faster you will go. Remember not to apply cunningham tension until you begin to bend the mast.

Playing the main in gusts and waves

As the wind builds or drops, alterations to mainsail shape must be carried out quickly to keep the boat performing at its full potential.

Light airs, wind 5-10 knots, building

Set the mainsail to its maximum depth. Then add a small amount of pre-bend by removing any chocks in front of the mast and replacing then behind the mast. This will help to open the leech and move the flow aft in the sail. Ease the cunningham right off and pull the outhaul about half-way out so that the bottom batten is not hooking to weather when the traveller is on the centreline.

Masthead rig Apply enough tension on the backstay for correct headstay tension and leave the runners and checks slack. As soon as the wind builds so much that you have the crew on the weather rail, begin to power up the sail. Put the chocks back in front of the mast and straighten it using runners and checks. Only when you have all crew members to weather and you begin to have excessive backwind should you begin to flatten the sail:
● Ease the runners and checks and increase cunningham tension.
● Increase backstay and sheet tension.
● Increase tension on the outhaul/flattener.

Fractional rigs Apply enough tension on the runners for correct headstay tension, leaving the checks and backstay slack. When the wind has built so much that the crew are on the weather rail, put the chocks back in front of the mast and straighten it using the checks. Only flatten the sail when all the crew are to weather and backwind is becoming excessive:
● Increase the tension on the runners and backstay.
● Ease the checks.
● Increase the tension on the cunningham, sheet and outhaul/flattener.

For either rig, gradually apply all these controls until they are at maximum and the sail is as flat as possible with full cunningham. Then change to the No. 2 genoa which will enable you to drop the traveller without increasing backwinding. From there go to the No. 3, then to the No. 3 with one reef, No. 3 with two reefs, No. 4 with two reefs and finally No. 4 with three reefs.

In gusts

A combination of rapid traveller control and backstay adjustment must be made to keep the boat at a constant angle of heel. If the boat is allowed to heel more than her current angle, the helmsman will have to use excessive rudder to stop her rounding up and the brakes will go on. As a gust hits, the traveller must fly down to leeward and stay down until the boat begins to come upright. Then the traveller must be hauled back up immediately to prevent the helm from going into neutral or reverse. If you have enough crew aboard the backstay can also be played, increasing the tension in the gusts and easing it in the lulls. Close liaison with the genoa trimmer is essential: he must be kept informed about the amount of backwinding, and he must respond immediately to your call by

moving the car aft or simply easing the sheet to keep the slot open and the boat moving fast. If the boat has excessive helm the brakes will be on and she will make a lot of leeway.

Above: Dump the traveller in a gust to reduce weather helm (left). As soon as the gust passes haul the traveller back to return the boom to the centreline of the boat (above).

Poor upwind performance can take two forms: either the boat will not point high enough, or it will point well enough but lacks speed.

Boat doesn't point

Poor pointing ability may mean that your boat simply won't point in the same direction as the boats around you. Alternatively, it may point in the same direction but make more leeway, so that when you go off the start line you drift to leeward and are forced to tack away from the next boat down.

Boat points low

1. Check that you have a small amount of weather helm.
2. Check that the genoa is in tight enough by looking at the telltales. Make sure they are all breaking together.
3. Check that the genoa car isn't too far forward. This will make the sail too full which in turn will create too full an entry.
4. Check that the backstay (runners on a fractional rig) is tight enough. If it isn't the genoa entry will again be too full.
5. Check that your mainsail has enough leech tension. If not, the leech of the sail will not be working and although speed will be good, pointing will suffer. A sign of this will be little or no weather helm. To cure the problem, bring the boom onto the centreline and then ease the backstay or increase the sheet tension – or both. Be careful not to stall the top of the sail by oversheeting.
6. Check that the mainsail is not too flat, resulting in a loss of power. If this is the case the slot will be too open. If there are 12 knots of wind or more you should be getting some backwinding in the mainsail. It is always a good idea to check your heel angle with other boats prior to starting. If they are heeling more they obviously have more power in their sails – always a good idea for getting off start lines where the apparent wind is down because everybody is 'pinching' and going slowly.

Too much leeway

In this case your rig is probably stalled out or you have too much or too little weather helm.

1. Check that your genoa isn't oversheeted. If it is you will be able to point high but you will go slowly and produce less lift off the keel, so you will drift sideways. Try easing the sheet a little, build speed and then try to point.

2. Check the tension on the backstay (runner on a fractional rig). You may have too much. Your genoa will have an entry fine enough for the wind to accept but you may in fact be going so high that the airflow isn't attaching itself to the sail's leeward side until maybe three or four feet behind the luff. On a masthead rig try easing the backstay to build more speed. On a fractional rig ease both the runners and the backstay.

3. Check that your boom is not above the centreline. If it is, the lower half of your mainsail leech will be stalled and you will go sideways as well as forwards. This is a common mistake, because in your efforts to point higher you bring the traveller further to weather to increase weather helm.

4. Check that the top telltale on the mainsail isn't stalled. The flow will be destroyed if the air isn't getting out of the head and a reduction in speed will be inevitable.

When a boat is to leeward, you must keep your distance to weather if you are to avoid having to tack off. This in itself makes you try to point higher to avoid her, and by so doing you obviously go slower. By going slower, you lose lift off the keel and begin to slip ever-so-slowly sideways. The boat to leeward then goes forward and gets closer, so you try to point even higher – and that is the end. In such a situation, do not try to out-point your opponent; instead try and match her for speed. Once you feel you are slightly faster begin to point higher. Never let her mast move further forward than your bow, for if it does you will have to tack away due to the lee bow effect.

Boat points well but is slow

This problem is also most evident at the start, when you go off the line and the boat to weather and behind sails right past you.

1. Try using more backstay (runner on a fractional rig) to straighten the headstay and make the genoa flatter. Increase the genoa halyard tension to drag the flow forward and make the leech straighter, reducing the amount of air being thrown into the mainsail.

2. Slide the genoa car aft to further flatten the genoa and open up the slot.

3. Check that you have no more than five degrees of weather helm. If you have more than this, the brakes will be on.

4. Cure the helm problem by checking that the traveller isn't above the centreline. Check that the bottom batten isn't pointing to weather; if it is then either drop the traveller or increase the outhaul tension. The latter is better because dropping the traveller will close the slot.

5. Try easing the runners and checks and increasing the cunningham tension to flatten and straighten the exit of the mainsail. Make sure you have enough twist up top by checking that the top telltale is just flying.

Fractional rig problems

Although the principles of sail tuning apply to both masthead rigs and fractional rigs, the control systems vary. Where a fractional rig is equipped with runners the basic variations given in the preceding pages apply, although some further points are noted on page 68.

Swept back spreaders and no runners

Fractional rigs without runners can be more of a problem.

Headstay

Without runners, achieving sufficient headstay tension is difficult. As the backstay is pulled on in an effort to increase headstay tension the topmast also bends. Because of this the maximum amount of headstay tension available is governed by the stiffness of the topmast. If the topmast is very flexible it is almost impossible to tension the headstay, because the mast just keeps on bending without increasing the tension significantly. Therefore it is essential to have a substantial amount of stiffness in the topmast to control headstay tension.

The distance between the hounds and the tip of the spar will also affect control over the headstay. If the distance is small, as on the J24, the problem is not as great as if the distance is large.

Control over the headstay is governed by:
- Backstay tension
- Shroud tension
- Lower shroud tension
- Mast stiffness

Backstay tension Increasing backstay tension increases headstay tension, reducing it will do the opposite.

Shroud tension Assuming your shrouds are set aft of the mast step, increasing their tension will increase headstay tension.

Lower shroud tension Increasing lower shroud tension will again hold the mast aft and increase headstay tension, providing they too are behind the mast step.

Mast stiffness Stiffening the mast will reduce bend. Increasing backstay tension will now increase headstay tension more effectively as the load will transfer more of its force into the headstay before the mast bends.

Mainsheet tension Increasing mainsheet tension will increase backstay tension while reducing it will do the opposite.

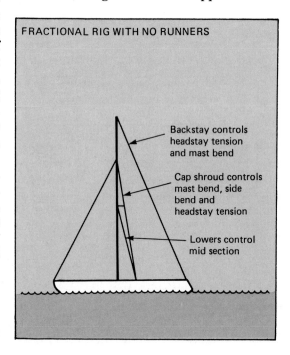

FRACTIONAL RIG WITH NO RUNNERS

Backstay controls headstay tension and mast bend

Cap shroud controls mast bend, side bend and headstay tension

Lowers control mid section

Mast bend

You now have an understanding of how to control headstay tension. However, your mainsail must be able to match your variable backstay settings.

For example, in the strongest winds you will be applying maximum backstay, so your mainsail must match the bend that is being forced into the mast. It will be no use keeping a straight headstay if by so doing your mainsail is inverted by an overbent mast. To achieve the perfect match you must adjust spreader angles and lower shroud tensions so that your mainsail sets perfectly when maximum backstay is applied. Increasing tension in the lower shrouds will stiffen the mast, as will angling the spreaders forward.

In light airs the reverse is the case because you will be using less backstay to keep the headstay straight. A reduction in lower shroud tension will then be desirable so that the mast can bend under less pressure.

Shrouds

The shrouds, apart from holding the mast up, control the following:
- Sideways bend
- Fore-and-aft bend
- Headstay tension
- Mast rake

If the main shrouds are tighter than the lower shrouds, the mast will bend more fore-and-aft. The mid-mast may also dip to leeward.

If the shrouds are slacker than the lowers, the mast will be stiffer fore-and-aft, and the section above the spreaders will tend to fall over sideways. To achieve a straight mast sideways, the two tensions must be properly matched.

Spreaders

Long spreaders give increased sideways stiffness, while spreaders angled forward give more fore-and-aft stiffness.

If you find that bending the mast to give the correct mainsail shape makes your headstay too tight, then either:
- Your spreaders are angled too far forward, making the mast over-stiff.
- The lowers are too tight, again making the spar too stiff.

Try easing the lowers and see if this helps, but watch out for the mast dipping to leeward in the middle. If this happens, your spreaders are too far forward.

If your mast is dipping to leeward at spreader height, with plenty of tension on the lowers, you may find that your spreaders are too long. Increasing tension on the lowers may cure the problem but it will also increase the stiffness of the mast. If this is undesirable then shorten your spreaders, half an inch at a time, until the mast is straight side-to-side without excessive tension in the lowers.

Lowers

The primary job of the lowers is to support the mast and prevent it from collapsing. They hold the mast from deck to spreader height, while the shrouds support it from spreaders to hounds. They prevent side bend, and because they are fixed at deck-level, behind the mast step, they also control fore-and-aft bend. If the mast bends, the lowers obviously become tighter and in doing so they stiffen the mast fore-and-aft.

Tuning the fractional genoa

Because the backstay cannot control headstay tension on a fractional rig as well as it can on a masthead rig, the genoa will have to be cut to allow for more headstay sag. The principles for sheeting and setting the sail are the same as described earlier except that the mainsail is a bigger and more critical sail to set. The genoa must therefore be tuned around the mainsail rather than the other way round.

Tuning the main

Because the main is a larger proportion of the total sail area its trim is paramount. The genoa has to be adjusted to cope with the mainsail setting. For example, if you need to drop the traveller, do so and ease the genoa sheet to accommodate it.

The mainsail must be cut to maximum length along the foot in its eased position so that when sailing offwind the clew reaches the black band. on the wind use the flattener to reduce the curvature in the base of the mainsail. This gives three to four inches extra foot length off the wind.

Reefing can be left later than on a masthead boat because you have more control of the main, and in any case reefing early results in neutral or even lee helm.

Fractional rig with runners and checkstays

On today's high performance yachts, greater control of the rig is provided by runners, checkstays and backstay controls. Because of this it is possible to set up the mast and sails without compromise.

Fore-and-aft bend is controlled by the runners, checks and backstay – leaving the shrouds, spreaders and lowers to hold the mast straight in the side-to-side plane. The shrouds will, however, give some support to the fore-and-aft bend via the spreaders: angling them forward will increase stiffness, while angling them back will reduce it.

The backstay's only function is to control fore-and-aft bend, particularly at the tip of the mast. The runners control headstay tension and downwind rake. The checks, together with the deck ram, control mid and lower mast bend.

Adjustments as wind speed builds from 5-20 knots apparent

Starting at five knots apparent wind, the runners will need to be well eased (depending on the genoa). You may have to pre-bend the mast to flatten the entry of the mainsail, and you may have to use some backstay to open the leech. Using backstay alone could give you sufficient headstay tension in these conditions.

As the breeze builds you must immediately increase runner tension to control headstay sag. In doing so you will automatically increase mast rake, so you will need to wind on more mainsheet and backstay to compensate. The checkstays will probably be attached to the runners so they will have to be eased as soon as the runner is tensioned, to prevent the mast from inverting. As you increase mainsheet tension, the mast will begin to bend and override the backstay. You can either leave the backstay slack or tension it again, depending on twist requirements. Remember that if you ease the mainsheet, you must also ease the backstay if you want to keep the fullness and twist constant. Likewise, if you ease the runners the backstay will become tighter.

It's worth using light gauge wire for the backstay, so that if you forget to ease it before the runners at the windward mark the backstay will break before the mast does.

Right: Many high-performance yachts use fractional rigs fitted with runners and checkstays to give maximum flexibility.

If you follow the advice given in the sections above your upwind speed should be blistering. Now let's make sure you gain places downwind too.

Reaching without a spinnaker in medium winds.

To achieve good speed on a reach in medium airs you must make the sails fuller and more powerful.

Having rounded the weather mark, ease the cunningham off completely and release the flattener/outhaul until you see vertical creases forming out of the base of the sail. Ease the vang until the top telltale is just flowing.

The more vang tension you use, the flatter and tighter-leeched the sail will become. A tight leech is desirable for two-sail reaching as it generates maximum power by preventing the air from escaping out of the sail too early. To achieve a tight leech you will need plenty of vang tension – but this will tend to bend the mast and de-power the sail. You must try to prevent this by using other means to hold the spar as straight as possible and maintain maximum power and speed.

Rake

Ease off the backstay, runners and deck ram so that the mast can rake forward. You should be looking for around ten degrees of forward rake, or enough to give you neutral helm. Once the runners have been eased, you can tighten the checks to reduce bend in the mast and power up the mainsail.

Balance

Every effort must be made to ensure that minimum rudder angle is being used in keeping the boat on track. You no longer require lift off the blade, so tune the sails for neutral or slight weather helm – one degree at most. The entire crew should be positioned as far aft and outboard as possible to reduce helm and keep the boat sailing on her full waterline length.

Genoa trim

As the genoa is eased out for the reach, the head twists open and the sail must be oversheeted in its base to keep the top working. Therefore move the fairleads forward to keep all three telltales breaking together. If the upper telltales break after the lower ones, the genoa car is too far forward.

Move the fairlead outboard as far as possible to increase the width of the slot.

Above: Good trim for a close reach. Note how the crew have moved aft, the genoa fairleads have been moved forward and outboard, and the other sail controls have been loosened.

This will enable the mainsail to be let out further before the genoa backwinds it. Ease the genoa halyard until horizontal creases appear out of the luff. This will move the flow aft and give the sail more fullness.

Light air adjustments

Basic settings for light air reaching are the same as for medium winds. If the wind drops very light, however, put more bend into the mast and keep the vang slack so that the air can move across the sail and escape from the leech without stalling. If the boom's weight is still holding the leech too tight, take a spare genoa halyard, fasten it to the end of the boom and use it to lift the spar and thus remove tension from the leech.

Get one of your crew to hold the clew of the genoa up, to keep the leech open and clear of the mainsail. The rest of the crew should move forward and to leeward to lift the stern clear of the water, thus reducing drag.

Heavy air adjustments

When the wind increases to 'overpowering' conditions – when the mainsail is eased out so far that backwinding occurs – it is time to flatten the sails off.

Pull the flattener on and return the rake and tension to their upwind settings. Ease the vang off until helm is returned to neutral and as a gust hits, ease both the genoa sheet and mainsheet. It is better to let the sails lift than to use excessive rudder. If you are still overpowered increase the genoa halyard and cunningham tensions and move the fairleads further aft to dump the head of the sail. Your last option, before reducing sail area, is to increase the backstay tension to flatten and twist the mainsail.

Left: Reaching with a standard genoa, using a barber-hauler to drag the sheet and clew of the genoa as far to leeward as possible to keep the slot open.

Staysail

The staysail is used to increase the flow over the mainsail when broad reaching – it can transform the main from a flogging mass of Dacron into a driving sail.

The ideal time to hoist the staysail is when reaching with the spinnaker pole just off the forestay (and the main boom eased at 60 degrees). Hoisting the staysail closes the slot, so the boom needs to be sheeted harder: this effectively powers up the mainsail.

Note that the staysail should not be used as extra sail area – the clew is set high because the sheet is led well aft to widen the slot. Low-cut staysails that fill the gap between the spinnaker and deck are ineffective.

The staysail can be set on very broad reaches in the same way, but the tack is then fixed to the weather toerail. As before, the aim is to give drive to the main, but in this case you also gain some sail area under the spinnaker which flies higher on a broad reach.

Remember to keep the luff of the staysail on the break and the leech driving. This will prevent the spinnaker being oversheeted.

When hoisting the staysail don't look for an increase on the speedometer – the best you can hope for is a length over four miles. It's hardly surprising that people usually leave the sail in its bag.

High clewed reacher

You may have a special reaching genoa on board. This will be an extremely full sail with a high clew, specially designed for two-sail reaching. The high clew enables the sail to be sheeted well aft, thereby moving the leech further outboard and increasing the slot width. Set the sail using the telltales as you would a normal genoa.

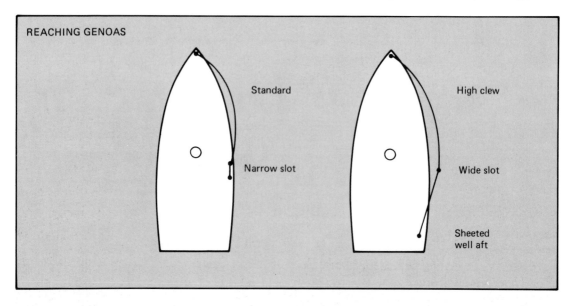

REACHING GENOAS

Standard

Narrow slot

High clew

Wide slot

Sheeted well aft

Setting a spinnaker

Wind strength will be the most important factor governing your choice of headsail or spinnaker. If you have 25 knots of breeze across the deck you will not be able to set a spinnaker if the wind is forward of abeam (90 degrees apparent or less). But if the wind is ten knots you will be able to set a spinnaker at angles as small as 60 degrees, depending on the shape of the sail.

Before arriving at the weather mark, try to work out what your apparent wind angle is going to be. If it is a marginal decision, then go round the mark with the pole set and the spinnaker ready to go. Settle onto your compass course and in medium airs you should be able to make the sail pay if the apparent wind angle is 75 degrees or more.

Spinnaker choice

The size of boat will determine the size of spinnaker and the cloth weight. Large 0.75 oz sails cannot take as much force as small sails. Your sailmaker should tell you how much apparent wind your spinnaker will stand. For example a 12-metre 0.75 oz sail will either distort or explode in 20 knots apparent, whereas a J24's kite will survive up to 30 knots apparent.

Bigger boats are also allowed to carry more sails in their inventory, making the correct choice vital. Assuming you have on board a 0.5 oz, 0.75 oz and 1.5 oz, and your boat is 35 feet long, you should use the 0.5 oz for running in wind speeds up to 15 knots true and reaching in 10 knots true (13 knots apparent). The 0.75 oz can be used for running in anything under 20 knots true (18 knots apparent), while the 1.5 oz is used for wind speeds above that. However, your 1.5 oz may be flatter than your 0.75 oz and therefore a better reaching sail. If this is so it will pay you to use it for reaching in anything over 12 knots apparent. The 0.75 oz is then used for broad reaching and heavy airs running and the 0.5 oz for light/medium running and light reaching.

Above: Use the vang (kicking strap) to adjust the trim of the mainsail. Here it is too loose.

Above: With too much tension on the vang the leech is too tight for reaching with a spinnaker.

Above: Correct vang tension ensures that the mainsail keeps its shape on the reach (and on the run).

Trimming for close reaching

When you eventually set the spinnaker the boat must be pre-set in anticipation of the sudden increase in sail area. To avoid a broach as the sail fills ease the vang off to reduce weather helm. Make sure the trimmer doesn't initially over-sheet the sail as this will almost certainly round you up. Begin to adjust the mainsail for maximum performance as soon as the spinnaker is set properly and all the crew are in position to weather.

Pole height

At whatever height you set the pole, be sure that it is parallel with the foredeck at all times to provide maximum extension from the mast. Any height adjustment at the outboard end must be matched at the inboard end.

Never set a spinnaker with the clew lower than the tack. Try to keep them level; if anything you should have the clew higher than the tack. When reaching treat the sail like a genoa; try to keep the leech open so that the air can escape without hindrance.

Once the pole has gone forward to the forestay, the only way it can now move – if the wind goes further ahead – is down. Say you have the clew and tack level with an apparent wind angle of 85 degrees. The wind goes forward to 75 degrees so you sheet harder. By sheeting harder, you drag the clew aft and down, forcing you to lower the pole to keep the tack level. Failure to do this will result in a closed leech with the flow well aft in the sail, and you will lose speed.

When reaching in long waves or changing winds the pole must be constantly adjusted to keep it level. If this is not practicable – as when surfing down waves, where the sheet is repeatedly eased going into the back of a wave and sheeted in going down the wave – set the pole so that the clew and tack are level when sheeted in and the clew is higher when eased.

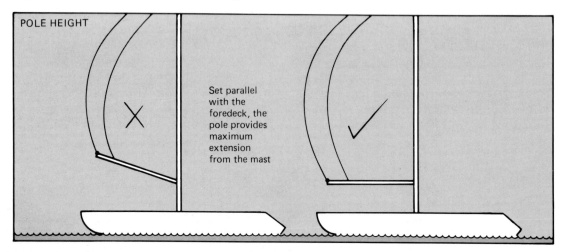

POLE HEIGHT

Set parallel with the foredeck, the pole provides maximum extension from the mast

Left: The pole is too high, so the clew is lower than the tack.

Left: The pole is too low, so the tack is lower than the clew.

Below: Adjusting the pole brings clew and tack level (far left), but raising the inboard end of the pole (centre and right) gives more projected area.

Pole angle

On a manageable close reach, set the pole one inch off the forestay so that the spinnaker is flown as far away from the boat as possible. Bringing the pole aft will increase the sheet tension and the sail will end up closer to the mainsail.

However, in broaching conditions (with mainsail flogging) it will pay to bring the pole back twelve inches or so. This will flatten the sail and move its centre of effort forward, releasing weather helm.

Sheet lead position

Arrange the spinnaker sheet fairleads so that when the sail is sheeted to its maximum, with the pole on the forestay, the sheet bisects the clew – that us pulling equally along the leech and the foot. The lead should also be as far outboard as possible to widen the slot between the spinnaker leech and mainsail.

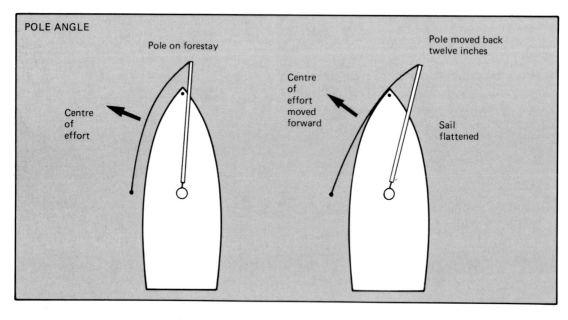

POLE ANGLE

Pole on forestay

Centre of effort

Centre of effort moved forward

Pole moved back twelve inches

Sail flattened

Trimming for maximum speed

The trimmer must be up to weather in a position where he can clearly see the luff of the sail. He should have the sheet on a weather winch, so that his winder can also operate from the windward side.

The sheet must be played constantly to accommodate every change in either compass heading, wind speed or wind direction. Close liaison between the trimmer and the helmsman is vital for the best results. The helmsman must call if he is altering course and the trimmer must inform the helm if the wind moves forward or aft of the beam. The spinnaker should be set with its luff constantly curling. If it isn't it will be oversheeted, and the result will be a closed slot and loss of speed. Anticipate boatspeed by sheeting in when accelerating and easing off when slowing down.

Telltales

Telltales on the luff and leech can be very useful. They should be positioned at four-foot intervals up the sail, one foot behind the tapes. Use them as you would use telltales on a genoa, playing the sheet so that the weather telltales on the luff are always breaking.

Right: Oversheeting the spinnaker closes the slot and reduces speed.

Spinnaker trim on a beam reach

When the wind is beind the beam – 90 degrees or more – you will want maximum power and projected area from your sails. The 0.75 oz reacher will probaly be your largest sail; set it in windspeeds of 9-18 knots apparent. If the sea is flat it will pay to keep it set in lower windspeeds, but if it is rough it will pay to go to a 0.5 oz at around 10 knots apparent. Because the 0.5 oz is lighter it will keep its shape better in waves, when the boat and rig are being thrown about. In flat water this isn't a problem; as long as the sail is taking up its shape the larger spinnaker should be set (down to around seven knots apparent).

Pole height and angle

Again try to keep the tack and clew level; if anything the clew should be higher. Judging the best pole height can be confusing. As you let the pole forward you must also ease the sheet to keep the luff curling. As the sheet is eased the clew rises so you must lift the pole to compensate. You can carry on doing this until you end up with the spinnaker flying up in the clouds. The opposite can happen when you start bringing the pole aft: in your efforts to keep the clew and tack level you end up with the sail down by the bow, strapped around the forestay.

You must get some idea of the sail's vertical profile. This is best done from off the boat, looking at the sail sideways-on. Ideally the centre seam of the lower half of the sail should lie parallel with the mast. If it is too low the base will 'tuck under' and the air will be unable to escape from under the sail. If the pole is too high too much air will escape and you will lose drive.

Another guide is to see where the spinnaker first 'breaks' along its luff. Ideally this should be just above half height. If it breaks higher then lower the pole; if it breaks lower, raise the pole.

Your last indication is to look at wind angle compared to mainsail angle. Without a spinnaker the mainsail will be set about five degrees ahead of the apparent wind. With a spinnaker up this should go to about ten degrees. If it is less than this the pole is too far forward, creating an over-wide slot. If it is more than ten degrees the pole is too far back.

Below: An excellent spinnaker profile with the centreline vertical at the foot.

Reaching in medium winds

To get the most out of your boat in medium winds, try the following:

1. Ease off the runners and backstay to bring the mast upright. If this makes the rig floppy, take a halyard to the bow and tension it.

2. Power up the main by easing the outhaul and cunningham.

3. Reduce bend in the mast by tensioning the checkstays and adjusting the vang properly.

4. Fly the biggest spinnaker you have on board.

5. Make sure the tack and clew of the spinnaker are level.

6. Adjust the angle of heel for minimum helm by moving the crew weight.

7. If you're *still* slow, check the cut of the mainsail and kite – they may be cut flatter than the sails used by the rest of the fleet.

Right: Play the main to ease the pull on the tiller. Here the main is pulled in too far, giving weather helm. If dumping the main has no effect, ease the vang (kicking strap) as well.

Reaching in light winds

Again, keep both tack and clew level. As the wind falls off the clew will drop because there is insufficient force available to lift the weight of the sail. You must then lower the pole: this will straighten the luff, leaving less unsupported cloth for the air to fill and support. Use the lightest of sheets because their weight alone may prevent the sail from lifting.

Reaching in strong winds

All crew members should be aft and to weather. One person should be on the vang, ready to release it in gusts. The main and kite must be played constantly to keep both luffs breaking. Check that the tack and clew of the spinnaker are level (in very strong winds the clew should be higher than the tack so the air can escape). Make sure the sheets lead as far aft and outboard as possible. Generally, treat the spinnaker like a genoa.

If you seem to be going really slowly, try the following:
1. Lower the pole.
2. Ease the vang.
3. Consider a smaller or flatter spinnaker.
4. Pull out the flattener to maximum.
5. Consider a different weight of spinnaker. A 1.5 oz (or Mylar) spinnaker will be faster than a 0.75 oz because it holds its shape better.
6. Consider dropping the kite and setting the No. 1 genoa or reacher.

Out of control

Heel is the cause of broaches. Reduce it by:
1. Flattening the main by pulling the backstay, winding on the flattener and tensioning the cunningham.
2. Dropping the pole and winching it aft (one foot off the forestay).
3. Checking the spinnaker sheet lead is as far aft as possible.

FAULTFINDER

Close reach – boat won't point

On a close reach you may have trouble pointing or holding the same course to the mark as other boats, because your spinnaker simply collapses.
1. Look to the design of the sail. It may be that it isn't designed for reaching. It may be an all-purpose 0.75 oz which will be fuller and wider in the head than a specific design, such as a starcut.
2. Check that the pole isn't too high. If it is, the leech will be closed and the flow will be too far back in the sail.
3. Have you enough vang on the mainsail? Unless you are overpowered you should use plenty of vang to hold the leech up. Without it you may have lee helm.
4. Try bearing away ten degres to set the spinnaker and then slowly bring the boat back on course, telling the trimmer to sheet in as you come up. When the foot of the sail becomes bar tight you are at its limit: if he sheets any harder you will rip the sail in half. He must let you know when that point has been reached, and you must then sail a course to the spinnaker's luff.

Close reach – boat points well but has no speed

1. Check that you have no more than five degrees of weather helm. If you have more, ease the mainsail out to get rid of it. Losing power from the main is better than dragging your rudder sideways through the water.
2. Check that the mainsail and spinnaker are not oversheeted. The spinnaker luff should be on the curl and there should be a tiny hint of backwinding behind the mast.
3. Make sure the bottom of the boat is clean. It is pointless tuning the boat and rig if she's been lying in the water for over three weeks.
4. Check the age of the spinnaker. If the sail has had a lot of use it may be too tired to perform well. A sure sign of this is when the leech tapes are tighter than the cloth, resulting in the nylon bulging behind the tapes; this gives a closed luff and leech. If you can't afford a new sail, get your sailmaker to replace the tapes.

Running

After the upwind grind it's a delight to bear away and dry off. But this is not the time to relax or concentrate on lunch – you've got to get that kite up and keep it full, and trim the main constantly. Your reward will be apparent when you get to the leeward mark.

Running in medium winds

1. Check that the crew weight is not too far aft or to leeward – the boat should be level when running.
2. Ease off the runners and backstay to bring the mast upright. If this makes the rig too slack, take a halyard to the bow and tension it.
3. Adjust the vang so the top batten is parallel to the boom.
4. Square the boom at right angles to the wind (most people oversheet the boom on a run).
5. Check that the spinnaker tack and clew are level. Raise the pole if the clew is higher than the tack, and lower it if the tack is higher than the clew.
6. Check that the pole is at 80 degrees to the wind.

Above: Running with the pole too far back.

Above: Here the pole is too far forward.

Above: The pole in the correct position.

Running in light winds

First check that you're not pointing too far downwind – if you need to reach to get up speed do so. This can mean the pole on the forestay and gybing through 100 degrees in the lightest airs. Aim to keep the sail filling at all times – whatever angle you have to sail.

As the wind goes lighter drop the pole (keeping it horizontal) so there is less unsupported cloth for the air to lift. Use the lightest sheet available (preferably Kevlar) so the clew is not weighed down.

By this time most of the crew will be forward and to leeward (around the mast) to lift the stern and reduce drag.

The boom can be lifted to prevent its weight closing the leech. To do this, either reverse the hydraulics or use a halyard as a topping lift.

Running in strong winds

If you are slow, try the following:
1. Check that your spinnaker is as big as possible.
2. Try raising the pole. This will lift the bow and prevent it burying.
3. Bring the pole aft until it is at about 80 degrees.
4. Make sure all the crew are as far aft as possible.

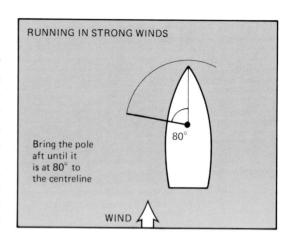

RUNNING IN STRONG WINDS

Bring the pole aft until it is at 80° to the centreline

80°

WIND

Out of control

If the boat begins to roll to windward ease the pole forward and sheet harder. If it rolls to leeward do the opposite.

Tension the vang until there is little or no twist in the main; insufficient vang will start the boat rolling.

The pole holds the tack of the spinnaker down, but the clew tends to sky. To prevent this pull down on the barber hauler to close the spinnaker leech; this lowers the clew and prevents the roll to windward; it works in the same way as the vang.

In extreme conditions set a small (2.2 oz) spinnaker. There is no need to peel – just drop the old kite and hoist the new one.

If the boat is dead downwind and starts rolling luff up ten degrees to steady her, then bear away under control.

FAULTFINDER

Poor speed on the run

1. Check that you have no more aft mast rake than the leaders.
2. See whether the faster boats are using bigger spinnakers.
3. Check the height and angle of the spinnaker pole.
4. If the wind is light, make sure the spinnaker is dry.
5. Try to use as little rudder as possible —too much and it will act as a brake.
6. Move the crew aft to help the boat surf, except in light winds when the crew should be forward to reduce drag.

Major surgery

If you have done everything you can to tune the rig yet the boat still performs badly, the problem may be more fundamental.

Keel shape

Check that the keel is symmetrical by using a wooden template. If it's not, ask the designer which side is correct and modify the other side by grinding off or filling in.

The keel must be aligned fore-and-aft, and it must be vertical. Run a string from a projection at the bow to the centre of the stern to check the alignment, and make sure it's vertical by measuring from each gunwale to the keel tip.

Poor speed in light airs can sometimes by cured by reducing keel weight, but upwind performance in a blow will suffer.

Rudder

Once you're certain the keel is correctly aligned, sight the rudder against it from aft. Check that there's no play in the bearings and make sure the blade is symmetrical.

If the boat is broaching a lot, consider a larger rudder.

On an IOR boat the lightest rudder gives the best rating advantage, so a carbon-fibre stock will rate better than an aluminium one.

Internal ballast

The lighter the construction of the boat the more ballast will be needed. The boat I'm sailing currently has 1.5 tons keel weight and nearly 1.5 tons of internal ballast. The ballast sinks the boat to its marks while gaining the maximum from the IOR.

Performance in a breeze or light airs can be improved by increasing or reducing ballast; trimming the boat by the bow will give a better rating, but it will make the boat slower and more tippy. The boat will of course have to be re-measured after ballast is moved.

Lightening the ends of the boat

If the boat goes slowly in a sea she may be heavy in the ends, particularly in the bow. Remove the toerails, fits a lighter pulpit or remove the toilet (!) to cure this. Note that moving anchors aft is illegal without re-measuring.

Lightening the mast

If performance is generally down, particularly in waves, check that you're not using a heavier mast than the opposition, or one with too high a centre of gravity. The latest IOR masts are double thickness at the bottom and single thickness at the top to reduce weight aloft.

It can sometimes pay to go for a larger, lighter section. This will give the same stiffness for less weight compared with a thin spar made of thicker metal.

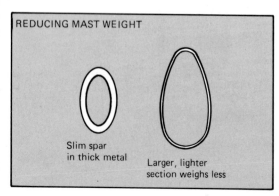

REDUCING MAST WEIGHT

Slim spar in thick metal

Larger, lighter section weighs less

Rating and performance

If you're competing in level rating events (such as half-ton races) the rule says that your boat must rate less than a certain limit. In practice you'll want to be spot on the limit. To reduce your rating reduce sail area, bump the hull and adjust the weight (and stiffness). Talk to your designer to achieve the best solution.

If you're competing IOR the sky's the limit! If, for example, you find yourself in the Admiral's Cup trials against six boats with the same rating as yours, you may decide to increase your rating to sail faster (and out into clear air). Alternatively you may decide to reduce your rating to finish behind the others and beat then on corrected time. The last thing you want is to be luffed or covered closely.

If you find your boat is more than adequte in light airs you can look to gain a rating advantage by reducing sail. But if you're a sparkling performer in strong winds it may pay to reduce the stability to lower the rating.

Personally I would prefer a fast boat without bumps that goes through the water well, and accept the rating as it stands rather than play the rule excessively.

In the same way, having tuned your boat during practice to the best of your ability, try not to be obsessed by boatspeed during the race. Nothing will put you further behind than going fast in the wrong direction, so concentrate on your helming, crewing and navigation. If a well-tuned boat was all that you needed to win a race, sailing would not be the sport that it is.

Go fast, have fun, and good sailing!

Fernhurst Books is the leading publisher of sailing books.
Please write, phone or fax us for a free full-colour brochure.

Fernhurst Books, Dukes Path, High Street, Arundel, West Sussex,
BN18 9AJ, England.

Phone 01903 882277 Fax 01903 882715